D1338002

SCOTTISH STEAM IN COLOUR

Hugh Ballantyne

Copyright © Jane's Publishing Company Limited 1987

First published in the United Kingdom in 1987 by
Jane's Publishing Company Limited
238 City Road, London EC1V 2PU

ISBN 0 7106 0403 3

All rights reserved. No part of this publication may be
reproduced, stored in a retrieval system, transmitted in any
form by any means electrical, mechanical or photocopied,
recorded or otherwise without prior permission of the
publisher.

Printed in the United Kingdom
by Netherwood Dalton & Co Ltd, Huddersfield

JANE'S TRANSPORT PRESS

Cover illustrations

Front: On the East Coast main line a recently ex-works Gresley A3 class Pacific No 60085 *Manna* (named after the 1925 Derby and 2000 Guineas winner) looks a beautiful sight in the afternoon sunshine heading towards the south end of Penmanshiel Tunnel with a down goods. No 60085 was built at Doncaster in 1930, was fitted with a double chimney in 1958, and acquired trough-type smoke deflectors the month before the picture was taken. This locomotive was withdrawn from service in October 1964. 7 May 1962. *(K M Falconer)*
Voigtlander Vito B Kodachrome II

Back: With the slack in the couplings taken up, Stanier Class 5 No 44898 is opened right up in full forward gear as she threads her way on to the down main line with a heavy limestone train and immediately faces a 10-mile unremitting slog up to Beattock summit from a standing start in Beattock yard. The necessary banking assistance in the form of Fairburn-designed 2-6-4T No 42694 can be seen at the rear, with the loco shed visible behind the banker. 31 May 1966. *(Hugh Ballantyne)*
Voigtlander Vito CLR f2.8 Skopar Agfa CT18 f4, 1/500

Right: A BR Standard Class 5 4-6-0 pilots a Gresley K2 class 2-6-0 round the horseshoe curve north of Tyndrum on the West Highland line with a Mallaig to Glasgow Queen Street train. June 1957.
(J M Jarvis)
Kodak Retina 1 f3.5 Ektar Kodachrome 8

INTRODUCTION

This is the last in a series of five volumes in which I have sought to portray through the medium of colour photography the latter days of everyday steam railway operation in the United Kingdom. The first four books each covered a BR region, and this generally enabled me to retain the corporate identity of each of the four grouped companies, but by geographical necessity this book of Scottish scenes covers the railways operated by both the London Midland & Scottish Railway (LMS) and London & North Eastern Railway (LNER) which between them controlled all the lines in Scotland from Whithorn in the south to Thurso in the north.

There had been five major Scottish railways, each with a fierce independence and great competitive spirit, and at grouping on 1 January 1923 the Caledonian Railway (CR), Glasgow & South Western Railway (GSWR) and Highland Railway (HR) went into the LMS system, whilst the LNER assumed control of the Great North of Scotland Railway (GNSR) and the largest of the Scottish railways, the North British (NBR). For ease of reference, except where it helps the narrative, the description of pre-grouping engines follows the classification given to them by the two big post-grouping companies and which continued in use by BR after nationalisation in 1948.

Again I extend my thanks to the photographers who have allowed the publishers and myself to include their now historic and quite irreplaceable transparencies, and for their foresight in using colour material when photographic equipment had a lesser degree of technical specification than today's cameras. Lenses were generally of lower resolution and colour film speeds were usually slower, so making exposures more difficult or the range of subjects more limited. This is one of the reasons why I have, where possible, included the details of the equipment and film used for making each picture, a feature which seems to have been appreciated by, and of interest to, many readers.

HUGH BALLANTYNE
Eccleshall, North Staffordshire
November 1986

A superb study of the low evening sun reflecting off HR 4-6-0 No 103 piloting GNSR 4-4-0 No 49 *Gordon Highlander* with the 'Scottish Rambler No 2' railtour as the train heads north through the remote country of the Galloway moorlands at Glenwhilly on the GSWR line from Stranraer to Ayr. 15 April 1963.
(Peter A Fry)
Kodak Retinette 1B   Agfa CT18

The best of Scottish scenery with an authentic one-off engine at work on its home line. On a beautiful spring day the only K1/1 class 2-6-0 No 61997 *MacCailin Mòr* leaves Glenfinnan station with the 1.00 pm restaurant car train from Mallaig to Glasgow Queen Street. This locomotive was built at Darlington in 1939 as one of six three-cylinder K4 class engines to Gresley's design, and was subsequently rebuilt at Doncaster in 1945 by Thompson with his standard two-cylinder layout and shortened version of his B1 class boiler. No more K4s were rebuilt but No 61997 was the prototype for seventy K1 locomotives turned out just after nationalisation in 1949-50. It was withdrawn in June 1961. March 1956.
(*J M Jarvis*)
Kodak Retina I
f3.5 Ektar Kodachrome 8

'Princess Coronation' class No 46244 *King George VI* has its tender topped up with water at the north end of Carstairs station during a stop whilst working a down express from Crewe. This engine was one of 20 'Coronations' allocated to English sheds and painted in maroon livery by BR, whilst their Scottish stablemates remained in the standard BR passenger livery of lined Brunswick green. Note the very distinctive style of the former Caledonian Railway Carstairs No 2 signalbox in the background, demolished when electrification was completed in 1974. 19 August 1961. (*K M Falconer*) *Voigtlander Vito B Kodachrome II*

Carstairs station fortuitously escaped the ravages of the BR 'rationalisation era', when many stations were either closed or had their facilities reduced to bus shelter mediocrity, and today still looks as attractive as it does in this view. The motive power and signals have gone though, and there is now 25 kV overhead equipment in place, but the scene looking over the wall of this island platform station remains basically as it was when 'Jubilee' class 4-6-0 No 45671 *Prince Rupert* entered the down platform with the 9.15 am (SO) Crewe to Glasgow Central train. No 45671 was built at Crewe in 1935 and withdrawn in 1963. 18 August 1962. (*K M Falconer*) *Voigtlander Vito B Kodachrome II*

The classic Edinburgh photographic location, a view from one of the footbridges in Princess Street Gardens with an unusually clean St Margaret's B1 emerging from The Mound Tunnel just after leaving Waverley with the 1.18 pm (SO) to St Andrews via the East of Fife line. By the time this picture was taken most services on this route were worked by DMUs but summer Saturday extras, such as this train, were still steam-hauled, with B1s predominating. No 61330 was built by North British in 1948 and when withdrawn in November 1963 went into service stock, becoming Departmental No 23. It was finally withdrawn in November 1965. 11 August 1962. *(K M Falconer)*
Voigtlander Vito B Kodachrome II

6

Gresley-designed V3 class 2-6-2T No 67668 approaching platform 7 at Edinburgh Waverley from Craigentinny carriage sidings with the empty stock for the 'Edinburgh & Dalkeith' railtour which it later hauled over most of that historic Edinburgh railway which opened in 1831. This scene at the east end of Waverley station changed greatly in the late 1970s when the 1937 colourlight signalling system was replaced and the track layout simplified. The train has just emerged from Carlton Tunnel and above it can be seen the ramparts of the former gaol, now surmounted by the government offices of St Andrew's House. A total of 92 of these useful passenger tank engines were built between 1930 and 1940, all at Doncaster. The first 82 were known as V1 class and the remaining 10 as V3, of which just over half were employed in the Scottish area. Those working in the Edinburgh area were mainly allocated to St Margaret's shed and their principal work was on the Musselburgh branch, the suburban lines and further afield down to Galashiels. Eventually DMUs took over their duties and by the end of 1962 their days in Scotland were over, although some of the English engines continued at work until 1964. The locomotive seen here was built in 1938, eventually reboilered to V3 in 1954 and withdrawn in 1962. 25 August 1962. (*K M Falconer*) *Voigtlander Vito B Kodachrome II*

Above: After general repairs at Darlington in March 1965, A4 class No 60019 *Bittern* rejoined the Ferryhill (Aberdeen) stud of streamlined Pacifics working out their last years in fine style on the Glasgow to Aberdeen three-hour expresses. This picture shows this lovely locomotive on what became a regular diagram for it in April of that year, the 5.30 pm Glasgow Buchanan Street to Aberdeen restaurant car express, the 'Saint Mungo'. Under a sky which threatens a storm, the express is passing Ballathie just before the dip in the line to a viaduct over the River Tay on the now-closed section of the Caledonian main line between Stanley Junction and Kinnaber Junction. 19 April 1965. *(Ken Plant)* *Agfa Silette Kodachrome II*

Right: One of the former King's Cross favourites, A4 No 60034 *Lord Faringdon* — the highest-numbered member of the class and by the time this picture was taken one of the eight A4 class survivors in Scotland — was recorded as performing well about this time. Here it crosses the River Allan at Dunblane one sunny summer evening with the 5.30 pm Glasgow Buchanan Street to Aberdeen express, the 'Saint Mungo'. 2 September 1965. *(Ken Plant)* *Agfa Silette*

Magnificent sight on the Mallaig extension of the NBR West Highland line shown to best advantage by means of colour photography with Gresley K2 class 2-6-0 No 61791 *Loch Lagan* piloting K4 class 2-6-0 No 61995 *Cameron of Locheil* up the 1-in-50 rise out of Glenfinnan station with the early morning 5.45 am restaurant car train from Glasgow Queen Street. On this occasion No 61995 had had difficulty in keeping time and the K2 was added at Glenfinnan to help the train, by then an hour late, to its destination and terminus of the line 24½ miles further on. April 1956.

(J M Jarvis)

Kodak Retina I f3.5 Ektar Kodachrome 8

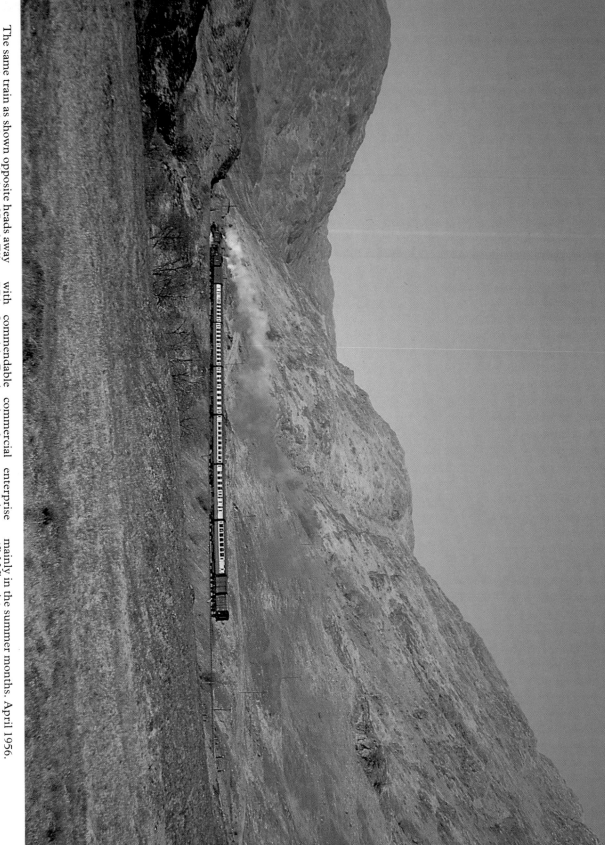

The same train as shown opposite heads away westwards towards the north side of Loch Eilt beyond which was the next stop at Lochailort. Thankfully this line is still open for traffic, and with commendable commercial enterprise BR's Scottish Region has been promoting steam-hauled excursions and other special trains between Fort William and Mallaig, mainly in the summer months. April 1956. (*J M Jarvis*). *Kodak Retina I f3.5 Ektar Kodachrome 8*

11

The attractive Fowler Class 2P 4-4-0s were used quite extensively on local services of the former GSWR lines in Scotland but here No 40644, fitted with a Midland-style chimney, stands in the sunshine somewhat off-course at Perth shed. Seen gleaming in its clean lined black livery, it was understandably being given an admiring glance by Vic Forster from Beeston, who in the 1950s and 60s was well known for organising interesting and highly popular annual tours to Scotland for East Midlands members of the RCTS. 27 May 1957.

(Peter W Gray)
Agfa Super Silette   Kodachrome

A beautifully turned-out Pickersgill Class 3P 'Caley Bogie' No 54485 seen at Perth shed. There were 48 engines in this class and they outlived the other Caledonian 4-4-0s which all traced their ancestry back to the McIntosh 'Dunalastair' class of 1896. From the 1950s much of their work was on passenger trains on the Highland section and all remained in service long enough to be painted in lined black livery. The last of the class was withdrawn in December 1962 and most regrettably none was saved for preservation. 1960.

(John Adams)

Above: An everyday occurrence in former times, now almost forgotten—an engine shunting a rake of loose-coupled wagons. NBR 0-6-0 J37 class No 64623 has not strayed far from its home shed at Dunfermline and is seen busy in the yard at Inverkeithing North Junction. These 0-6-0s were introduced by W P Reid and known as NBR Class S; 104 were built between 1914 and 1921. They were handsome locomotives and their 5 ft coupled wheels enabled them to be found on all types of goods work and, at busy times, on passenger services. The first was not withdrawn until 1959 and the last four survived until April 1967, only a month before the end of steam in Scotland. 7 May 1966. (*R Hobbs*)

Agfa Silette BL f2.8 Color Solinar Kodachrome II

Right: Thompson B1 class No 61324 lays a thick trail of smoke over the triangle at Inverkeithing as it wheels the 10.30 am Millerhill (Edinburgh) to Dundee goods round to the East Junction prior to tackling the undulating section of line through Fife towards the Firth of Tay. 4 September 1965. (*Ken Plant*)

Kodachrome II

Left: An Autumn morning on Beattock incline as Stanier Class 5 No 45122 battles up a 1-in-74 section of what in steam days was a formidable 10-mile incline of gradients averaging 1-in-76. It is seen at Greskine Forest, approximately half way up, assisted at the rear by Fairburn 2-6-4T No 42192. 11 October 1963. (*Hugh Ballantyne*)

Voigtlander CLR   50mm f2.8 Skopar
Agfa CT18   f5.6, 1/500

Above: On an extremely hot morning, one of Beattock shed's bankers, Fairburn-designed 2-6-4T No 42694, going about its task assisting

Class 5 No 45176 as it toils to keep a mineral train moving towards Greskine signalbox about half way to the summit. 31 May 1966. (*Hugh Ballantyne*)

Voigtlander CLR   50mm f2.8 Skopar
Agfa CT18   f4, 1/500

This gem of a picture shows a lovely little NBR 0-6-0 goods engine of class J36 No 65243 *Maude* going about the regular daily job which it performed for over 30 years, the 'Ferry Goods' turn. This was a daily trip working from Edinburgh to South Queensferry via Ratho and Kirkliston, and this picture shows *Maude* with the return working about to pass under an approach span of the Forth Bridge at Dalmeny. No 65243 was built by Neilson & Co in 1891 to a Matthew Holmes design and was one of 168 locomotives in the class, of which 123 entered BR service in 1948. No 65243 first went to Haymarket shed in June 1928 and stayed there until that shed closed in 1964, then spent two years at Bathgate until withdrawn in 1966. *Maude* was named after a General from the First World War, Major General Sir Frederick Stanley Maude of the Coldstream Guards, who had a distinguished career including service in the Dardenelles and Mesopotamia before dying of cholera at Baghdad in 1917. Twenty-four others of the class also carried names associated with the Great War in recognition of the fact that they were requisitioned by the government and sent to France in 1917 for service on the Western Front. The South Queensferry branch closed in February 1966 but this gallant little engine has been preserved by the SRPS. To the pleasure of thousands, and with the co-operation of BR Scottish Region, it makes quite regular appearances on ScotRail lines. 22 March 1963.

(K M Falconer)
Voigtlander Vito B
Kodachrome II

One of Dundee's Peppercorn A2 class Pacifics No 60530 *Sayajirao* (named after the 1947 St Leger winner) coming through North Queensferry station with the 12.10 pm (ThSO) 1948 and withdrawn in November 1966. The Dundee Tay Bridge to Stratford Carpenter's Road goods. This was a regular job for a

Dundee A2 or V2 at the time (see also page 43), and this shed kept the engines for it in good condition. No 60530 was built at Doncaster in station at North Queensferry, situated on the East Coast main line between the Forth Bridge

and the tunnel at the top of the 1-in-70 gradient from Inverkeithing, is still open and enjoys a frequent service of trains to and from Edinburgh. 3 July 1965. (*K M Falconer*) *Voigtlander Vito B Kodachrome II*

In the late-1950s, to the everlasting joy of enthusiasts and thousands of people who have an affinity towards railways in general, BR Scottish Region returned four locomotives to traffic in pre-grouping livery, mainly for special workings. Of the five Scottish companies only the GSWR was not represented, as all its engines had been withdrawn before nationalisation. Here is the fine North British

example, restored in original livery as No 256 *Glen Douglas*, passing Rumbling Bridge station on the Devon Valley line between Kinross Junction and Alloa with a 'Scottish Rambler' tour. Near here the River Devon comes through a ravine which is spanned by three bridges, the oldest of which is a narrow arch dating from 1713. No 256 was one of 32 engines built at Cowlairs Works to William

Reid's design as Class K. All were named after glens and on grouping in 1923 they became LNER Class D34. This locomotive was built in 1913, repainted in NBR livery in August 1959, and has been preserved on static display in the Glasgow Transport Museum. 13 April 1963. (*R Hobbs*)

Agfa Silette BL   f2.8 Color Solinar Kodachrome II

The representative of the GNSR amongst the four restored Scottish pre-grouping engines was No 49 *Gordon Highlander*. This was one of eight locomotives built to the design of T E Heywood in 1920-21 as Class F. These locomotives were similar to 13 earlier non-superheated 4-4-0s of Class V, and both became LNER Class D40 at grouping. These eight engines were the final development of the

4-4-0 type on the GNSR and all were given attractive names, this one after a famous regiment with its headquarters in the same city as the railway, Aberdeen. In a part of the world where it was said 'ye're nae a sojer if ye're nae a Gordon,' No 49 was always known as 'the Sojer'. In this splendid picture it comes under a tall three-arch bridge on the 1-in-80 climb up to Cleland on the former CR Glasgow to

Edinburgh direct line with the 'Scottish Rambler No 4' railtour on a gorgeous spring day. No 49 was built by North British in 1920 and eventually went into the Glasgow Transport Museum on static display in 1966. 13 April 1963. *(R Hobbs)*

Agfa Silette BL   f2.8 Color Solinar
Kodachrome II

Left and below: Apart from the solitary Class 8 Pacific No 71000, the 10 'Class 6 'Clan' Pacifics were numerically the smallest BR Standard class of locomotive, so there are correspondingly fewer good pictures available to illustrate them. These two photographs help redress the balance, and well portray No 72009

Clan Stewart in active service. This engine was one of five allocated to Carlisle Kingmoor shed and is seen leaving Carstairs with the 9.25 am Crewe to Aberdeen, one of the last regular daily steam-hauled passenger turns on the West Coast route. In the winter timetable the train terminated at Perth, but in summer a

portion ran forward to Aberdeen. No 72009 was built at Crewe in 1952 and withdrawn after a mere 13 years service in 1965. None of the class has been preserved. 1 August 1964. (*KM Falconer*) *Voigtlander Vito B   Kodachrome II*

Above: Portrait of a rather rakish-looking NBR passenger tank locomotive designed by Reid and classified M. The company, somewhat unusually, placed the order for building with an English contractor, Yorkshire Engine Company of Sheffield, for 30 engines which were delivered between 1911 and 1913. They became useful machines working mainly suburban traffic around Edinburgh and Glasgow, but eventually were to be found all over the NBR system on short passenger turns. They became LNER Class C15 and most were withdrawn by 1956 but two, including this one, No 67474, seen at Eastfield shed Glasgow, survived until April 1960. 28 May 1959. (*R C Riley*)

Agfa Super Silette f2 Solagon Kodachrome 8

Right: A vintage portrait of former Caledonian Railway Class 0F 0-4-0ST No 56025 resplendent in BR lined black livery shunting at St Rollox Works, Glasgow. These little engines, known as 'Pugs', were built for use on sharply curved tracks. A total of 39 were constructed by the Caledonian between 1885 and 1908 to the designs of Dugald Drummond (including this one) and John McIntosh, and 14 came into BR stock in 1948. The last survivor was withdrawn in 1962. 31 May 1952. (*T B Owen*)

Leica IIIc f2 Summitar Kodachrome 8 f3.5, 1/60

Left: BR Standard Class 5 No 73107, built at Doncaster in 1955, is seen working flat out just north of Greskine signalbox on Beattock incline, banked by Fairburn 2-6-4T No 42192, as they give their all to get a northbound iron ore train up to the summit 4½ miles further on. 10 October 1963.

(Hugh Ballantyne)
Voigtlander CLR 50mm f2.8 Skopar
Agfa CT18 f4, 1/250

Above: In the early morning sunlight Class 5 No 45061, one of the 1934-built Vulcan Foundry series in the first batch of this large class comprising 842 locomotives, pounds up the 1-in-69 and steepest part of the long Beattock incline near Greskine cottages with a northbound fitted goods. 30 May 1966.

(Hugh Ballantyne)
Voigtlander CLR 50mm f2.8 Skopar
Agfa CT18 f4, 1/500

Left: Coming south on the now closed and lifted NBR line from Bridge of Earn just south of Perth to Kinross, there was a stiff climb of 1-in-75 for six miles through the Ochil Hills, the effect of which can be seen by the mighty effort being expended by 'Austerity' 2-8-0 No 90596 of Thornton Junction shed as it approaches the summit of the line close by Glenfarg station. 27 August 1966. (*R Hobbs*)

Agfa Silette BL   f2.8 Color Solinar   Kodachrome II

Above: With the splendid backcloth of the Ochil Hills rising sharply out of the valley of the River Devon, Gresley 0-6-0 J38 class No 65929 from Dunfirmline shed climbs the steep gradient beyond Tillicoultry station on its way to Alloa from Dollar Colliery with a loaded coal train. When this picture was taken this was the only remnant of the Devon Valley line open for goods traffic, as the rest of this NBR branch from Alloa to Kinross was closed to passengers in June 1964. 28 May 1966. (*R Hobbs*)

Agfa Silette BL   f2.8 Color Solinar   Kodachrome II

One of Scotland's most photographed lines was the little Caledonian Railway branch which ran from Killin Junction, on the main line from Callander to Oban, down to Loch Tay station situated at the western end of the long and deep (in some places over 500 ft) loch of the same name, a distance of 5 miles. The 1 mile section from Killin to Loch Tay was closed to traffic in 1939, but as the shed was situated there the line continued in use for access to and from it. In this picture BR Standard Class 4 2-6-4T No 80092 comes down the valley of the River Dochart towards the attractive little town of Killin with the 2.46 pm from Killin Junction. Sadly the branch and its main line from Callander to Crianlarich Lower were put up for closure from 1 November 1965, but closed prematurely on 28 September of that year due to a rock fall in Glen Ogle. 6 July 1965. (*R Hobbs*) *Agfa Silette BL f2.8 Color Solinar Kodachrome II*

High Noon at Loch Tay and on a sunny spring day all is quiet at this delightful railway backwater. In the distance Caledonian Class 2P 0-4-4T No 55204 raises steam outside its shed in readiness for the next spell of activity up to Killin Junction, whilst in the foreground a small Fordson van, like the engine long since disappeared, is prominent outside the neat little station which by then was used as a private dwelling. 17 May 1961. *(Michael Mensing)* *Retina IIa f2 Xenon Agfa CT18 f8, 1/100*

Left: The attractive setting of 'Bonnie Dundee' is evident one fine summer morning as Stanier Class 5 No 44908 approaches the city with the 9.15 am Glasgow Buchanan Street to Dundee Tay Bridge train. The bowling green, visible on the right of the picture, is indicative that bowls is a popular pastime — there seen to be bowling greens in nearly every Scottish town and village, certainly far more than in their English counterparts. 2 September 1965. (*Ken Plant*) *Agfa Silette Kodachrome I*

Below: Throughout its history the NBR relied on 0-6-0 locomotives for the haulage of goods and mineral traffic, and this picture shows a typical goods train at Dundee Tay Bridge hauled by Reid-designed J37 class No 64615. These engines were the final development of 0-6-0 by the old company and 104 were built between 1914 and 1921, initially coming into service during the First World War when traffic was heavy. They competently hauled long-distance goods and mineral trains over all the North British system. 8 June 1962. (*T B Owen*) *Leica M2 f2 Summicron Kodachrome II f2.8, 1/250*

Above: Amidst the rural setting of the 4¼-mile branch to the terminus at Leslie, a Gresley J38 class 0-6-0 No 65909 shunts the trip working from Markinch. This had brought traffic for the paper mill of Smith & Anderson Ltd, providing the reason for running the train. The J38s were a Gresley 4 ft 8 in wheel design of which 35 were built at Darlington, all within the first five months of 1926. They were sent to Scotland for use on main line goods work and short-distance mineral haulage in the Fife and Lothian coalfields and industrial Midlothian.

The subsequent Gresley 0-6-0 design, Class J39, had larger wheels making it a more versatile locomotive. Nevertheless the J38s, despite high coal consumption, were free steamers and very strong haulers. They never moved from Scotland and spent most of their lives allocated to only four sheds. They were the last LNER-built class to remain intact (until December 1962) and upon withdrawal of the last two in April 1967 they had the melancholy distinction of being the last Gresley-designed locomotives in service. The engine

seen here survived until November 1966. 2 September 1966. *(Les Nixon) Exakta Varex IIa 50mm Pancolar Kodachrome II*

Right: The same engine on the same duty at Markinch, the main line junction for the Leslie branch, just north of Thornton Junction, where this locomotive was shedded. 1964. *(Peter J Robinson) Kodak Retina IIc f2.8 Heligon Ektachrome*

Left: With the blue waters of Loch Ryan in the background, Stanier Class 5 No 44935 heads away from Stranraer Harbour station with the 1.40 pm train over the former GSWR 'Port Road' to Dumfries. 12 July 1963. *(Michael Mensing)*
Kodak Retina IIa *f*3.5, 1/500
Agfa CT18 *f*3.5, 1/500 *f*2 Xenon

Above: One of the 1947 Horwich-built Stanier Class 5s, No. 44999 looking quite neat and tidy in lined black livery, stands outside the rear of Stranraer shed receiving some light repairs to its motion. This engine survived until 1966, in which year no less than 171 members of the 842-strong class were withdrawn. 7 September 1964. *(Hugh Ballantyne)*
Voigtlander CLR *50mm f2.8 Skopar*
*f*8, 1/60

37

Left: Thompson B1 class 4-6-0 No 61029 *Chamois*, one of the batch of 40 named after species of antelope, working hard on the 1-in-88 climb out of Montrose on the short single line section to Usan as it heads south with the 12.20 pm Aberdeen Craiginches to Dunbar cement empties. In the background the Montrose basin is visible, a tidal lagoon through which the River South Esk flows into the sea. No 61029 was built at Darlington Works in 1947 and withdrawn in December 1966. 31 August 1965. (*Ken Plant*) *Agfa Silette Kodachrome*

Above: A carefully selected location and a fine summer's evening have combined to produce this most attractive picture of Class 5 No 44998 crossing Bridge No 325 east of Carmont signal-box on the 1-in-102 climb up from Stonehaven with the 5.30 pm (SX) Aberdeen to Perth train. At the time this duty was booked for an A4 Pacific, but this particular engine appeared again the day after this picture was taken, perhaps covering for an A4 stopped for minor repairs. 31 August 1965. (*Ken Plant*) *Agfa Silette Kodachrome II*

The 'one off' Gresley K4 class 2-6-0 No 61997 *Cameron of Lochiel* with the distinctive odd-shaped left-side steam pipe cover clearly visible (also see page 52), heads a Fort William to Mallaig train across the impressive curved Glenfinnan viaduct on the North British Mallaig Extension line. This structure, like most major bridges on the Mallaig Extension, is of pre-stressed concrete, a construction technique first employed extensively on this line by contractor 'concrete Bob' McAlpine. March 1956. *(J M Jarvis) Kodak Retina I f3.5 Ektar Kodachrome 8*

The early BR corridor passenger stock livery stands out well in the winter sunshine as a train hauled by a BR Standard Class 5 piloting an LMS Stanier Class 5 passes some of the fine scenery of the West Highland line on the long 1-in-67 climb east of Tulloch towards remote Corrour. The train is the 7.40 am Mallaig to Glasgow Queen Street with restaurant car attached at Fort William. March 1956.

(J M Jarvis)

Kodak Retina I   f3.5 Ektar   Kodachrome 8

Gresley A3 class Pacific No 60072 *Sunstar* (named after the 1911 Derby winner) has apparently been given a somewhat menial task of hauling a coal train, seen coming out of the down goods loop at Newhailes Junction, on the East Coast main line east of Edinburgh at the point where the Musselburgh branch turned away. The A3 and its train had been looped to allow 'Deltic' No D9000 priority passage on the down 'Flying Scotsman' from King's Cross. No 60072 was a longstanding Gateshead and later Heaton (Newcastle) engine, and at one time was a regular performer on the 'Queen of Scots' Pullman express between Newcastle and Edinburgh. 28 April 1962.
(*K M Falconer*)
Voigtlander Vito B   Kodachrome II

A clean Dundee Gresley V2 class 2-6-2 No 60973 approaches Millerhill Yard, situated on the east side of Edinburgh astride the Waverley route to Carlisle, with the 12.10 pm (ThSO) Dundee Tay Bridge to Stratford ((ThSO)) Dundee Tay Bridge to Stratford Carpenter's Road goods (see also page 19). The scene here has now changed completely and although the running lines remain open for goods traffic the vast Millerhill Yard and its two shunting humps, opened in 1962, is now closed. The track in the down yard has gone and the up yard is only used for non-revenue traffic by the Civil Engineer. Finally, the view behind the train has been blocked by the high embankment of the Musselburgh by-pass road, 19 June 1965. (*K M Falconer*) *Voigtlander Vito B Kodachrome II*

Left: On a warm late-spring day BR Standard Class 7 Pacific No 70005 (formerly *John Milton*), in the filthy external condition common in the 1960s, was running fast at the foot of Beattock incline and about to shoot past the yard and station trailing a line of vans heading south towards Carlisle. On the right the track of the short Moffat branch can be seen curving away out ot the picture. This had been closed to all traffic on 6 April 1964. 31 May 1966.

(Hugh Ballantyne)
Voigtlander CLR 50mm f2.8 Skopar f4, 1/500

Above: At Elvanfoot the main line of the old Caledonian Railway, now part of the electrified West Coast main line from Glasgow to London, turns away from the upper Clyde valley and enters sparsely populated upland country near the Lowther Hills. This little station was the junction for the former Wanlockhead and Leadhills light railway, but by the time this picture was taken of BR Standard Class 4 2-6-0 No 76098 pulling out with a pick-up goods from Carstairs to Beattock, most traces of the branch had disappeared and today there is virtually no evidence that a railway junction and station existed in this exposed windswept upland location. 30 May 1966.

(Hugh Ballantyne)
Voigtlander CLR f2.8 Skopar Agfa CT18 f5.6, 1/250

45

Left: In a beautiful setting on the Caledonian line from Stirling to Perth, Gleneagles station is today the only one to remain open between Dunblane and Perth, and even by the time this picture was taken the branch to Crieff had been closed for two years and the track and crossovers leading to the platform to the left of the picture removed. Even so on this lovely bright day it was a treat to see a clean 'Black 5' No 44794 leaving the station with the 1.30 pm Aberdeen to Glasgow Buchanan Street train.
28 May 1966. (*R Hobbs*)
Agfa Silette BL
f2.8 Color Solinar
Kodachrome II

Right: Coming up the rising 1-in-100 gradient past the site of Auchterader station towards the summit near Gleneagles, with the afternoon sun bathing the northern slopes of the Ochil Hills in the background, Gresley A4 class No 60019 *Bittern* is running well with an up Aberdeen to Glasgow three-hour express. When this picture was taken the A4s were down to five and this engine, together with No 60024 *Kingfisher* both allocated at Aberdeen Ferryhill shed, were the last two in regular line service. The great era of these streamlined Pacifics came to an end on 14 September 1966.
28 May 1966. (*R Hobbs*)
Agfa Silette BL
f2.8 Color Solinar
Kodachrome II

Above: A rural scene on the 10¼-mile Kirkcudbright branch in south-west Scotland as BR Standard Class 4 2-6-4T No 80023, built at Brighton in 1951, approaches Castle Douglas with the 9.30 am from Kirkcudbright. 18 July 1963. *(Michael Mensing) Voigtlander Bessa II f3.5 Heliar Ektachrome High Speed f5.6, 1/500*

Right: On the same branch a wooded setting south of Tarff, the only intermediate station, is provided for Stanier Class 5 No 44957 on the last stages of the journey with the 6.08 pm from Dumfries. Trains serving the branch not only ran to Castle Douglas for main line connections but some, such as this, conveniently continued to Dumfries, the largest town in the area. The branch was closed to passengers on 1 May 1965, and like the main line between Dumfries and Stranraer closed completely shortly afterwards on 14 June 1965. 19 July 1963. *(Michael Mensing) Voigtlander Bessa II f3.5 Heliar Ektachrome High Speed f5.6, 1/500*

In the summer of 1965 the last three remaining Peppercorn A2 class Pacifics Nos 60526/30/32 were allocated to Dundee but were somewhat unpredictable in their workings as many of their jobs were on standby or goods turns (for example see page 19). No doubt the photographer on this occasion was well pleased to see No 60530 *Sayajirao* nice and clean working the 10.00 am Dundee Tay Bridge to Glasgow Buchanan Street train. Here the Pacific is setting off from Gleneagles at 10.55 with its train of eight coaches and one bogie van, next stop Dunblane and due Glasgow, 47½ miles on, at noon. Note that the attractive brass engraved Doncaster maker's plate, No 2021 of 1948, is clearly visible on the cabside under the number. 30 August 1965. (*Ken Plant* Agfa Silette Kodachrome)

In sparkling condition Peppercorn A2 class No 60532 *Blue Peter* (the 1939 Derby and 2000 Guineas winner), then one of three A2s remaining in service in Scotland, leaves the cathedral town of Dunblane on an overcast spring day with the 1.30 pm Aberdeen to Glasgow Buchanan Street train. During 1966, in the last summer of LNER Pacific running, this engine was quite often used on this train, returning to Aberdeen on the 11.02 pm, and was regarded as a free-running and powerful locomotive. No 60532 was built at Doncaster in March 1948, named a year later, and was the last A2 in service, being withdrawn in December 1966. This fine engine has been preserved privately, but has never been seen any main line running. It is to be hoped that one day it can be put back into BR-approved condition and some of its old exploits recaptured for all enthusiasts to see. 16 June 1966. (*R Hobbs*)

Agfa Silette BL f2.8 Color Solinar Kodachrome II

51

One of the six K4 class 2-6-0s designed by Gresley for use on the West Highland line of the North British section of the LNER. These engines were improved performers compared with the K2s which up to that time were the mainstay of the line and capable of hauling 220-ton passenger trains unaided. When the first K4, No 3441 *Loch Long*, entered traffic in 1937 it came up to expectations by hauling 300-ton trains unassisted. With their greater power and climbing ability, the K4s were hard-slogging engines but their downfall was on the level sections at the Glasgow end where higher speeds were required: their 5 ft 2 in coupled wheels and three-cylinder arrangement meant that the middle big ends tended to work loose and nut-tightening was a frequent necessity. In 1959 the K4s were transferred from Eastfield to Thornton Junction, and their West Highland days were finished, but this picture shows No 61995 *Cameron of Locheil* back at Fort William shed, its home depot between 1939 and 1954, having worked in on an SLS special train over the West Highland line. One interesting minor feature visible here is that this was the only member of the class with an odd-shaped outside steam pipe on the left side only. After this last appearance, No 61995 went back to Thornton Junction and was eventually withdrawn in October 1961. 18 June 1960. (*G W Morrison*)
Zeiss Contaflex   f2.8 Tessar   Agfa CT18

At that extreme outpost of the former LNER system, the Mallaig terminus of the West Highland line of the NBR, the enginemen are having a job to get J37 class 0-6-0 No 64636 round on the turntable, whilst sister locomotive No 64536 patiently sits in the sunshine watching the performance. Behind can be seen the waters of the Sound of Sleat. 1 June 1963. (*Douglas Hume*)

The rolling countryside of Ayrshire seen in its beautiful spring colours belies the fact that there was an extensive coalfield in the region which gave rise to much railway traffic. Although steam in the area was entering its last summer when this picture was taken, Hughes Mogul No 42919, built at Crewe in 1930, looks in good trim having received attention at Cowlairs Works a few weeks before, as it nears Annbank Junction with load of coal from Killoch Colliery situated on the GSWR branch which once ran to Belston Junction.

Steam working finished at Ayr in October 1966 but at least this locomotive survived until the very end. 3 May 1966. *(R Hobbs)*
Agfa Silette BL   f2.8 Color Solinar
Kodachrome II

Traversing remote moorland country in Galloway, Class 5 4-6-0 No 44675 has just passed the isolated station of Gatehouse of Fleet and line summit with the 3.50 pm Stranraer Town to Dumfries train. This engine was fitted with Skefko roller bearings on its coupled axles, and no doubt this made it more comfortable for the crew as it starts to drift down the 1-in-76 gradient for some miles towards Big Fleet viaduct. Gatehouse of Fleet station had the dubious honour of having just about the poorest train service in the country. The 1961 timetable, for example, showed that only five trains a week called there and of these four were down trains and only one, at 12.31 pm on Saturdays, was in the up direction! This very scenic line between Dumfries and Challoch Junction, 6½ miles east of Stranraer, was closed to all traffic on 14 June 1965. 16 July 1963. (Michael Mensing). Voigtlander Bessa II f3.5 Heliar Ektachrome f5.6, 1/500

Left: Caledonian 0-4-4T Class 2P No 55124 pulling away from Oban with the 4.55 pm branch train to Ballachulish. 18 May 1961. *(Michael Mensing) Hasselblad 1000F f2.8 Tessar Agfa CT18 f3.5, 1/500*

Above: Double-headed Class 5s Nos 45400 and 45443 make an impressive departure from Oban with the 5.15 pm to Glasgow and Edinburgh. This train also conveyed a through sleeping car to Euston with an arrival in London next morning at 7.55. Also for some years in the summer the train had an observation car attached between Oban and Glasgow. 19 May 1960. *(Michael Mensing) Kodak Retina IIa f2 Xenon Agfa CT18 f3.5, 1/500*

57

Very close to the border in Dumfriesshire, the North British had an attractive little branch which left the Waverley route at Riddings Junction and ran 7 miles to Langholm, a small market town nestling in the valley of the salmon-laden River Esk. This is a typical scene of later days with a two-coach train hauled by an Ivatt-designed Class 4 2-6-0. No 43139 of Carlisle Kingmoor shed was a longstanding favourite on this branch, but here sister engine No 43011 is seen at the single platform making ready to leave on the 3.28 pm to Carlisle. The branch lost its passenger service in June 1964, and closed completely in October 1967. The site of the station has been redeveloped as a council housing estate. 10 October 1963.

(Hugh Ballantyne)
Voigtlander CLR   50mm f2.8 Skopar
Agfa CT18   f5.6, 1/60

On the Waverley route, Thompson B1 class No 61244 *Strang Steel* draws out of St Boswells, then in the county of Selkirk, from which branches once radiated eastwards to Reston and Tweedsmouth, with the 4.10 pm Edinburgh Waverley to Hawick local train. This engine was built by North British in October 1947 and two months later it was one of 18 in the class to be named after a director of the LNER. This was to commemorate the passing of the company, nationalised by the government of the day along with the other three grouped companies on 1 January 1948. Because of the length of some of the directors' names, the letters on the nameplates were only 3in high against 4in letters of the other named engines in the class. 10 September 1964.

(Hugh Ballantyne)

Voigtlander CLR   50mm/2.8 Skopar Agfa CT18   f5.6, 1/125

Left: The 1.00 pm from Mallaig to Glasgow Buchanan Street and London King's Cross leaving the Mallaig line at Mallaig Junction, Fort William, double-headed by Peppercorn K1 class 2-6-0 No 62034 piloting Thompson B1 class 4-6-0 No 61342. This train conveyed through carriages and restaurant car from Mallaig to Glasgow, plus through coaches and sleeping car from Fort William to King's Cross, giving an arrival in London next morning at 7.39 am. 20 May 1961. *(Michael Mensing)* *Hasselblad 1000F f2.8 Tessar Agfa CT18 f4, 1/500*

Right: Another Fort William scene as K1 class No 62052 backs some vans onto the 5.45 am Glasgow to Mallaig, prior to coupling up and working the train out to Mallaig. This train had originated as the 7.30 pm from King's Cross overnight sleeper to Fort William, but as with the corresponding up train, referred to above, the restaurant car worked between Glasgow and Mallaig. Seventy K1 class engines were built in 1949-50, all by North British, this one appearing in November 1949 and after only a short working life was withdrawn in December 1962. About the time this picture was taken, Fort William had six of the class, Glasgow Eastfield one and the remaining 63 were based at English sheds. 25 May 1961. *(Michael Mensing)* *Kodak Retina IIa f2 Xenon Agfa CT18 f3.8, 1/500*

Above: A general view at the former NBR shed at St Margaret's, Edinburgh, situated on the east side of the city. Facing the camera are B1 class No 61344, BR Standard Class 4 2-6-4T No 80055, and Gresley-designed V2 class 2-6-2 No 60846. The shed code in BR days was 64A and it was closed on 22 April 1967.
Agfa Silette BL   f2.8 Color Solinar   Kodachrome II

Right: Stanier Class 5 No 44924 making a circuitous approach to Edinburgh from the east side with the Edinburgh portion of the

9.40 am (Sun) train from Liverpool Exchange to Glasgow and Edinburgh. On weekdays the destination of this train was the Caledonian station at Princes Street, but from May 1962 that station was closed on Sundays and services from Carstairs diverted at Slateford to Waverley via Craiglockhart Junction and the Edinburgh suburban line, adding about 20 minutes to the journey. Princes Street station was completely closed on 6 September 1965 when the present direct link to Waverley was opened. This vantage point is known to local enthusiasts as 'The Bridge' and was regarded

in steam days as one of the busiest railway locations in Edinburgh. On the right can be seen the entrance to the vast Craigentinny carriage sidings, and on the left the goods lines between Craigentinny and Portobello Yard which at the time were very busy with local freight and light engines moving from nearby St Margaret's shed and the yards at Niddrie, Portobello Meadows and later Millerhill. These goods lines were taken out of use in 1967 and now there are only two running lines at this point. 12 August 1962. (*K M Falconer*)
Voigtlander Vito B   Kodachrome II

On the NBR East Coast main line to Berwick-upon-Tweed, a clean Thompson B1 class 4-6-0 No 61324 catches the morning sunshine coming up the 1-in-96 gradient between Cockburnspath and Grantshouse with an SLS 'Scottish Rambler' special train. This B1 was built in Scotland by North British in June 1948 and was withdrawn in October 1965. 14 April 1963. (R Hobbs)

Agfa Silette BL   f2.8 Color Solinar Kodachrome II

64

A picture which captures the atmosphere of the old NBR Waverley route which ran from Edinburgh to Carlisle via Hawick as the line climbs through the Southern Uplands on its way south. In sparsely populated high moorland country the railway climbed continuously from the textile town of Hawick for 11 miles at gradients around 1-in-80 through

Whitrope Tunnel to the summit seen here at the lonely Whitrope Sidings signalbox. Gresley V2 class No 60835 comes past the box with an Edinburgh Millerhill to Carlisle goods, starting the descent to Newcastleton. Regrettably this famous route was completely closed in January 1969, some years after the infamous Dr Beeching had ceased to be BR

Chairman, but the government of the day still permitted the closure policies introduced by him in the early-1960s to persist and the railway network continued to contract. 8 July 1965. (R Hobbs)

Agfa Silette BL   f2.8 Color Solinar
Kodachrome II

The NBR East of Fife line ran partly along the north side of the Firth of Forth, and in this scene on the branch Thompson B1 class No 61132 is coming across the viaduct to the east of the station at Largo. At the time the picture was taken the passenger service had gone and only the section from Leven to Crail remained open for goods; even this ceased in July 1966. Largo is a small town and port and perhaps its claim to fame rests in the fact Alexander Selkirk (better known as Robinson Crusoe) was born at Lower Largo in 1676. 16 June 1966. (R Hobbs)
Agfa Silette BL   f2.8 Color Solinar Kodachrome II

Just north of Perth, from its junction at Strathord, there was a short 3-mile branch which ran to Bankfoot known as the Bankfoot Light Railway. The branch lost its passenger train service in April 1951 but here 11 years later a special train organised by the SLS is seen approaching the little terminus station on a lovely spring day. The motive power was also interesting as Class 3F 0-6-0T No 56347 was formerly a Caledonian Class 782 engine in a series built from 1898 to a McIntosh design which became that company's standard shunt-ing engine. This locomotive was included amongst the last survivors withdrawn in 1962. 23 April 1962. (R Hobbs) *Agfa Silette BL f2.8 Color Solinar Kodachrome II*

The splendid Caledonian single-wheeler No 123 built by Neilson & Co in 1886 to a Drummond design needs no introduction, but this picture shows to excellent advantage the elaborate lining detail, particularly on the tender, of this elegant engine. No 123 is on the turntable at Oban having come out from Glasgow Queen Street with NBR 4-4-0 *Glen Douglas* on the Caledonian route via Callander. The photographer noted at the time that the loco staff at Oban spent much more effort in cleaning and servicing the Caley engine whilst on shed and gave the 'foreign' locomotive NBR *Glen Douglas* only the minimum of attention that decency required—and this 39 years after the grouping! 12 May 1962. (*G W Morrison*) *Zeiss Contaflex f2.8 Tessar Agfa CT18*

A busy scene at the crossing station of Arrochar & Tarbet close by the west side of Loch Lomond on the NBR line to Fort William. BR Standard Class 5 No 73077 with the 10.15 am Glasgow Queen Street to Fort William train watches Stanier Class 5 No 44973 piloting No 44956 into the station heading south with the 6.30 am from Mallaig to Queen Street. This station is still open and is now also used by trains to Oban which join the original CR line at Crianlarich. 13 August 1960.
(G W Morrison)
Zeiss Contaflex f2.8 Tessar Agfa CT18

69

A4 class Pacific No 60004 *William Whitelaw* (named after the first Chairman of the LNER who held office until 1938) has steam to spare as it comes under the roof at Perth station and slows to a halt with the 7.10 am Aberdeen to Glasgow Buchanan Street Express. 25 June 1964.
(Alan Wild)
Kodak
Retinette 1A
Perutz C18
f4, 1/250

Streamlined Pacific No 60007 *Sir Nigel Gresley* running hard past Cove Bay with the 7.10 am Aberdeen to Glasgow Buchanan Street express and going well on the rising grade with a driver who gives the impression he was all set to maintain the tight three-hour schedule for the 154 mile journey. No 60007 was one of six A4s which continued at work

into 1966, but it was the first casualty of that year, being withdrawn in February. Fortunately that was not the end of the story for No 60007 as it was purchased by the A4 Loco Society and sent to Crewe Works for restoration. In 1967, back as No 4498 in LNER garter blue livery. *Sir Nigel* made several runs on BR lines including a visit to the Southern

Region. Following the relaxation of BR's ban on steam in 1971, this locomotive has been foremost amongst the first division engines in steam and continues to give pleasure to very many people as it runs over the various approved BR routes in England. September 1964. (*J B Bucknall*)

Pentax S1 f2 Takumar   Agfa CT18

71

Left: A beautiful winter sight on the main line from Perth with BR Standard Class 6 Pacific No 72006 *Clan Mackenzie* nearing the summit of the 1-in-100 climb in the deep cutting south of Gleneagles station with the 12.10 pm Perth to Euston express. At the time this train was a regular job for a Kingmoor (Carlisle) engine, 'Princess Coronation', 'Clan' or 'Britannia' classes being most frequently used. Half the 'Clan' class, Nos 72005-09, were allocated to Kingmoor at this period. 20 February 1964.

(*K M Falconer*)
Voigtlander Vito B   Kodachrome II

Above: After struggling through a raging blizzard on the climb up Glen Ogle from Balquhidder, Caledonian Single 4-2-2 No 123 rests at Killin Junction with the two preserved Caledonian coaches during the course of the SLS Easter 1963 'Scottish Rambler' tour from Glasgow Central to Callander and Crianlarich

and then back to Glasgow via the West Highland line. This remote station closed with the rest of the Callander to Crianlarich section of the Callander & Oban line in September 1965. These four-day 'Scottish Rambler' Easter tours were a well-remembered feature of the Scottish railway scene in the early-1960s. Oh that ScotRail would reintroduce them for the early-1990s — what a roaring success they would be! 11 April 1963. (*K M Falconer*)
Voigtlander Vito B   Kodachrome II

73

Out of a class total of 842 Stanier Class 5 4-6-0s, only five allocated in Scotland received names and of these No 5155 *The Queen's Edinburgh* was only so named for two years from 1942. The remaining four all had attractive regimental names associated with Glasgow and the surrounding area and continued the very pleasant naming tradition of the LMS. This portrait shows No 45157 *The Glasgow Highlander* at its home depot of St Rollox brewing up in readiness to going off shed. No 45157 was built by Armstrong Whitworth at Newcastle-upon-Tyne in 1935, named in 1936 and withdrawn in 1962. 12 August 1960.
(G W Morrison) *Zeiss Contaflex f2.8 Tessar Agfa CT18*

From the NBR terminus at Glasgow Queen Street there is a severe 1-in-45 climb of over a mile out of the station up Cowlairs incline, and here two Glasgow Eastfield engines battle with this formidable start to their journey on the 10.15 am train to Fort William. BR Standard Class 5 No 73109 looks quite smart in lined black livery piloting Thompson B1 No 61355, which although in the same livery had not recently seen the cleaning gang. On the left the ECS of the all-Pullman 'Queen of Scots' is going downhill into Queen Street prior to its departure at 11.00 am to Newcastle thence via Harrogate and Leeds to King's Cross. 11 August 1960. (G W Morrison) Zeiss Contaflex f2.8 Tessar Agfa CT18

No doubt a stirring sound as well as sight as 3-cylinder 'Converted Royal Scot' No 46142 *The York and Lancaster Regiment* digs in her heels past Lamington in the upper Clyde valley with still 12 miles to go on the long climb towards Beattock summit at the head of the 10.50 am Glasgow Central to Liverpool Exchange and Manchester Victoria. No 46142 was one of the batch of 50 'Royal Scots' built by North British Loco Co in 1927, eventually converted with a 2A taper boiler in 1951 and withdrawn in 1964. From 1928 to 1934 it carried the name *Mail*. 14 October 1961. *(Derek Cross)*

Stanier 'Jubilee' Class 5XP No 45588 *Kashmir*, one of a batch of 50 'Jubilees' built by North British in 1934-35, and at the time allocated to Carlisle Kingmoor shed, looks a treat standing at Lockerbie station on the Caledonian main line to Carlisle. Although the locomotive was a familiar sight on this line, the train was not the ordinary service train it looks to be. This was in fact an enthusiast special organised by the SLS, and was about to run to Stranraer via the closed line through Lochar-briggs to Dumfries and then onwards through Castle Douglas and Newton Stewart. 14 April 1963. (*R Hobbs*)

Agfa Silette BL   f2.8 Color Solinar
Kodachrome II

77

Above: Once an everyday sight, on a crisp spring day Caledonian Class 2F 0-6-0 No 57261 was going about its business of working a light pick-up goods train, photographed passing Bridge of Allan station. When this picture was taken, the timeless scene was drawing to a close. No 57261, its three remaining sisters and four Caley Class 3F 0-6-0s were all withdrawn in November 1963, and were the last of 1070 Caledonian engines handed over to the LMS at grouping on 1 January 1923. As designed, these 0-6-0s were most attractive little engines but the appearance of over 170 of them, including this one, was radically altered for the worse by later fitting of the ugly stove pipe chimney. 12 April 1963. (*Peter A Fry*) *Kodak Retinette 1B Agfa CT18*

Right: On a bright summer's evening Stanier Class 5 No 45465, built at Crewe in 1938, brings the 9.25 am from Crewe to Aberdeen close by the North Sea coast on the high ground near Stonehaven. 9 August 1963. (*Peter A Fry*) *Kodak Retinette 1B Agfa CT18*

A historic colour picture of D40 class 4-4-0 No 62278 *Hatton Castle* taken at Kittybrewster shed, Aberdeen, in the year it was painted in BR lined black livery. This livery should be compared with the GNSR pre-1914 green livery which was applied to No 49, see page 21. In their time these engines worked the most important passenger trains between Aberdeen, Keith and Elgin. Eventually they were superseded by some English immigrants from East Anglia in the form of B12 class 4-6-0s which down graded them to branch line work, in particular the Craigellachie to Boat of Garten line through Speyside. No 62278 was built by North British in 1920 and named after the residence of G A Duff, the then Deputy Chairman of the company. This locomotive was withdrawn in July 1955. 4 September 1949. (*J M Jarvis*) *Kodak Retina I f3.5 Ektar Kodachrome*

At Aberdeen Kittybrewster shed a Holden ex-Great Eastern inside-cylinder Class B12/4 No 61508 in the lined apple green livery of the LNER makes a gorgeous sight standing in the yard. Between 1931 and 1943 a total of 25 B12s migrated from England to work on the Great North of Scotland section, gradually being released as the new B17 'Sandringhams' were delivered to the GE section as their more powerful successors. In Scotland the B12s took over the main services between Aberdeen and Elgin and other lines in the north-east of the country, performing well and carrying out the heaviest duties until the Thompson B1s made their appearance in 1947. The GNS section B12s were repaired locally at Inverurie Works and after the Second World War 20 of the 25 B12s were painted green as seen here, although after vesting day in 1948 the LNER lettering changed to BR and five digit numbers were applied, although retaining the Gill Sans characters.

Altogether 80 B12s were built to Holden's design and this one emerged from Stratford Works in 1913. It was withdrawn in 1953 but fortunately the last survivor of the class, No 61572, was privately purchased after withdrawal in 1961 and is now kept, albeit not in running order, on the North Norfolk Railway.

3 September 1949. *(J M Jarvis)*
Kodak Retina I   f3.5 Ektar   Kodachrome 8

Spring on the Highland line to the Far North at The Mound Junction. This little Peter Drummond design of 0-4-4T, No 55053, is shunting the dining car that had worked up on the 6.40 am Inverness to Wick train and was detached here in readiness for placing on the southbound return train to Inverness which had left Wick at 8.35 am and would stop here at 11.31 am. This delightful little engine was one of four built by the HR, only two of which survived to enter BR stock in 1948. Their job was to shunt at The Mound and work the 7¾ mile branch to Dornoch, a quiet seaside resort noted for its miles of sands and two golf courses. No 55053 was withdrawn in January 1957 after the branch had been upgraded to take the weight of BR Standard Class 2 2-6-0s. More surprising was the reallocation of a Western Region 0-6-0PT No 1649 to Helmsdale shed, and this also worked the branch including the last train on 11 June 1960.

May 1956. (J M Jarvis)
Kodak Retina I f3.5 Ektar Kodachrome 8

A scene at Achnasheen station on the Kyle of Lochalsh line, more or less half way between Dingwall and Kyle and situated in some remote country in the area of Ross & Cromary. Although only serving a tiny village, this station is a railhead for bus services to Wester Ross and gateway to some fine Highland scenery. In this picture the tail of the local bus can just be seen by the signalbox as the 10.45 am from Kyle of Lochalsh to Inverness hauled by Stanier Class 5 No 45361 comes into the up platform. Easter 1957. (*J M Jarvis*) *Kodak Retina I f3.5 Ektar Kodachrome 8*

Above: Heading for home on the last stages of the journey for the 'Down Postal' from London, Streamlined A4 class No 60034 *Lord Faringdon* comes round the curves towards Cove Bay, south of Aberdeen, just after 7.00 am on a bright summer morning. June 1965.

(J B Bucknall)
Pentax S1   f2 Takumar   Agfa CT18

Right: Stanier Class 5 No 45115, built by Vulcan Foundry in 1935, pours out the smoke as it comes under one of the impressive signal gantries at Ferryhill on the start out from Aberdeen with a parcels train to Perth. Note the first vehicle is a postal painted in the brighter red livery then used on some BR stock. September 1964. *(J B Bucknall)*
Pentax S1   f2 Takumar   Agfa CT18

The shed building and setting have a Scandinavian air about them but the engine betrays the fact that this is Ballachulish, to the west of Glencoe in the Highlands. Caledonian Class 2P 0-4-4T No 55263, nicely groomed, basks in the Spring sunshine whilst being prepared to work the 3.57 pm train to Oban. This was one of 10 post-grouping engines built by Nasmyth Wilson in 1925 to a design of J F McIntosh originating in 1900 as the Class 439 passenger tank engine. 3 April 1961. (*Ken Plant*) *Agfa Silette Kodachrome 1*

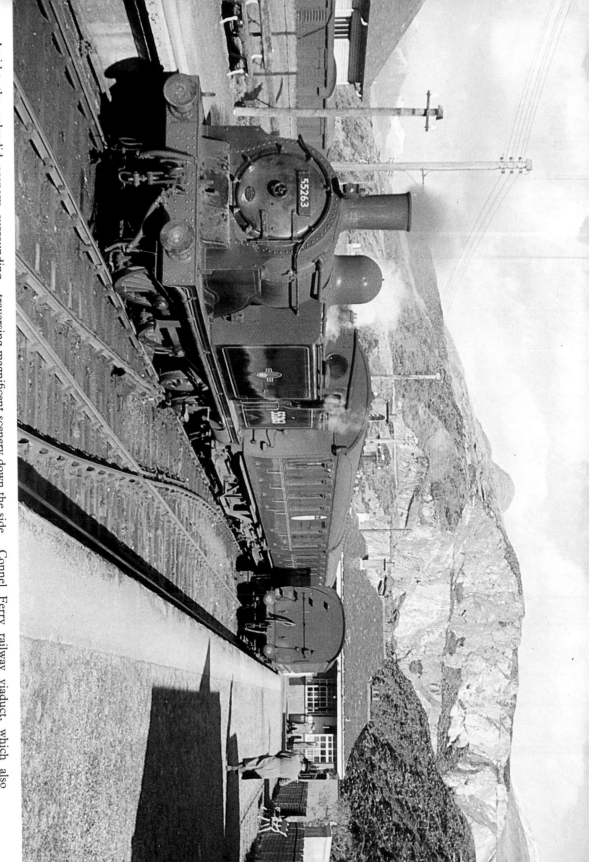

Amidst the splendid scenery surrounding Ballachulish on the banks of Loch Leven, Class 2P 0-4-4T No 55263 makes ready to leave the station with the 3.57 pm train to Oban. This was a journey of some 34 miles traversing magnificent scenery down the side of Loch Linnhe towards Connel Ferry, where connection was made with the line from Crianlarich for the last 6¼ miles into Oban. The Ballachulish branch was closed on 28 March 1966 and

Connel Ferry railway viaduct, which also carried a single track public toll roadway, has now become entirely a toll-free road bridge. 3 April 1961. (Ken Plant) *Agfa Silette Kodachrome I*

The Highland Railway livery adorning David Jones-designed 'Big Goods' 4-6-0 No 103 stands out well against the background of Inverness shed as the engine sits on the turntable. This locomotive was one of 15 built by Sharp Stewart & Co in 1894. They were the first 4-6-0s to run in Great Britain — amazingly, as the wheel arrangement was already well established on foreign railways and many of the type had been built by UK contractors for overseas customers. No 103 was withdrawn by the LMS for preservation in 1934 as No 17916 and returned to traffic in restored HR livery in 1959. It is now resident in the Glasgow Transport Museum on static display. 24 April 1962. *(Norman Glover)* *Voigtlander Vito B 50mm Skopar Kodachrome II*

Buchanan Street. 15 July 1957.
(*John Edgington*)
*Voigtlander Vito B f3.5 Skopar
Kodachrome I f4, 1/100*

Impressive departure from Inverness as two Stanier Class 5s, the leading engine being No 45123, get under way passing Welsh's Bridge signalbox with the 3.40 pm train to Glasgow

An interesting vintage and rare colour photograph of an engine from a class that led a very restricted albeit useful life shunting the dock lines at Aberdeen. This is Class Z4 0-4-2T No 68191 seen going about its business on the quay outside the Aberdeen Steam Navigation Co's offices. This locomotive was one of a pair ordered by the GNSR from

Manning Wardle of Leeds in August 1915, and which duplicated a similar order to the same makers in January of that year. This was because the first pair, being 5 tons heavier, were found to exceed the specified weight for locomotive haulage in the docks. Nevertheless all four worked from Kittybrewster shed and the first-built pair, classified Z5 by the LNER,

later found similar employment to their Z4 stablemates. This engine was the first of the Z4 pair to be withdrawn in 1959, and its twin No 68190 only survived another year. The two Z5s went in 1956 and 1960.
12 September 1958. (R Hobbs)
Balda Baldinette f2.8 Cassar Ilfordcolour

In the first decade of the 20th Century the increasing number of fast goods trains being run by the various British railways gave the incentive to Churchward on the GWR and Gresley on the GNR to develop the 2-6-0 type to operate such traffic in preference to the army of 0-6-0s then so employed. On the GNR, Gresley's first design was a 2-6-0 which appeared in 1912 and, after modifications, he produced a total of 75 locomotives classified by the LNER as K1 and K2. The eight K1s were subsequently reboilered as K2, and the class became a useful mixed traffic engine. In 1924 six went to Scotland. By 1932 a further 20 had gone north and after the Second World War the total reached 30. The engines in the Scottish area were fitted with larger side-window cabs and the cab roof was extended back 9in to give added protection against the northern weather. Also, in 1933-34 the 13 K2s which

regularly worked over the West Highland line received names of Lochs. This picture shows No 61790 *Loch Lomond* at Keith shed. One of the last batch of 25 built by Kitson & Co at Leeds in 1921, it was withdrawn in 1959 and although most had gone by 1960 one survived until 1962 but none have been preserved. 8 June 1957. (*T B Owen*)

*Leica IIIc   f2 Summitar   Kodachrome 8
f3.2, 1/60*

Scene at Stirling taken from the overbridge near the station showing the last-built Gresley A4 Pacific No 60034 *Lord Farringdom* leaving with an Aberdeen to Glasgow train. This was the 35th A4 built, emerging from Doncaster Works in July 1938, and was named *Peregrine*. Just after nationalisation in 1948 it was re-named to commemorate the last Chairman of the GCR and one of the original LNER directors. A much-liked engine at King's Cross Top Shed, following that depot's closure in June 1963 No 60034 was subsequently one of nine A4s transferred from England and first put into store at Galashiels and then at Bathgate. But by the Spring of 1964 it was back in service with its sisters for the 'Indian Summer' of main line A4 work which lasted two years and brought enthusiasts from all over the country to ride behind them on the Glasgow–Aberdeen road. 7 May 1966. *(R Hobbs) Agfa Silette BL   f2.8 Color Solinar Kodachrome II*

Kelty, in the north of Fife on the NBR line from Perth to Edinburgh via Kinross, was a focal point for numerous colliery branches and consequently was a busy junction and yard. In this picture Thompson B1 class No 61340, built at Gorton in 1948, comes south out of the sidings with a goods train up the sharp 1-in-80 gradient towards Cowdenbeath with banker Class J38 No 65907 tender-first pushing hard at the rear. Kelty station, just visible in the distance, was closed to passengers on 22 September 1930 but until the 1960s coal traffic kept the line busy, so much so that Dunfirmline shed supplied four engines daily for shunting, trip working and banking. The through route between Cowdenbeath and Hilton Junction, south of Perth, closed to passengers on 4 January 1970. The last goods line went later that year and now this once busy railway location has completely gone. 16 April 1965. (K M Falconer)
Voigtlander
Vito B
Kodachrome II

93

Above: A substantial station was built by the Caledonian Railway at Crieff to cater for holiday traffic to this attractive part of Perthshire and the resort and tourist centre the town provided. Crieff is in the valley of the River Earn and remains a popular centre but the railway has gone, the branch to Perth closing in 1951 and the line on which this train ran south to Gleneagles in 1964. Stanier Class 5 No 44979, built at Crewe in 1946, stands in the station which is still painted in its old LMS brown colours, with the stock ready to form the 2.45 pm train for the 9 mile journey to Gleneagles. 21 August 1963. (*Russell Leitch*) *Agfa CT18*

Right: The most north-easterly line of the NBR was a 13 mile branch from Montrose to Inverbervie, a small fishing port on the North Sea coast which once also had flax and rayon mills. This picture well illustrates the daily pick-up goods train heading south one afternoon back to Montrose with J37 class 0-6-0 No 64608 in charge passing the attractive fishing village of Gourdon, 1¼ miles from Inverbervie. The branch lost its passenger service in October 1951 and was closed to all traffic in 1967. 8 July 1964. (*Michael Mensing*) *Nikkorex F f2 Nikkor   Agfa CT18 f5, 1/250*

A splendid sight to stir Caledonian Railway enthusiasts at Perth station as two 4-4-0 'Caley Bogies', Nos 54485 and 54486, prepare to leave with a special train as a preview run for some filming sequences which were later shot on the Highland line to Aviemore. Note on the right the horseboxes, once provided by all the railway companies in great numbers for this lucrative traffic, but all swept away by BR during the period of retrenchment in the 1960s. 1960. (*John Adams*)